EXPLORE TOGETHER

Resource Book

Copyright © Scripture Union
First published 2017
ISBN 978 1 78506 568 2

British Library Cataloguing-in-Publication Data: a catalogue record of this book is available from the British Library.

Printed in India by Nutech Print Services - India

Cover and internal design by Jake Howe.

Scripture Union is an international Christian charity working with churches in more than 130 countries.
Thank you for purchasing this resource. Any profits from this book support SU in England and Wales to bring the good news of Jesus Christ to children, young people and families and to enable them to meet God through the Bible and prayer.

Find out more about our work and how you can get involved at:
www.scriptureunion.org.uk (England and Wales)
www.suscotland.org.uk (Scotland)
www.suni.co.uk (Northern Ireland)
www.scriptureunion.org (USA)
www.su.org.au (Australia)

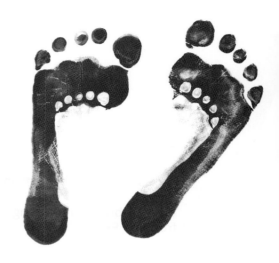

Contents

How to... Explore Together

Within our faith communities there is a rich diversity of God's people, all at different stages in their faith development and spiritual experience, and all with different learning needs and preferences. We are a beautiful collection of artists, scholars, reflectors, dancers, data collectors, fact finders, readers, sculptors, writers, musicians, actors, talkers and listeners.

Explore Together places the Bible at the centre of this diversity. It is a new and practical tool for helping people to explore God's Word and hear his voice in a way that embraces their natural preferences. It encourages the community to come together to share their thoughts, questions and revelations with each other. Any and all are welcome and there are no barriers to participation.

At the heart of Explore Together is a desire to see people hear from God and learn more of his love for them. It works with big groups, small groups, mixed-age groups, single-age groups, older people, young people, children, families, house groups, church congregations, youth groups, school groups... In fact, Explore Together can be used in any environment with any group dynamic. It is grounded in years of research and tried and tested in a multitude of contexts.

This resource book is designed to equip you and your community as you adventure, journey and grow with God. On this page and the next we have a few suggestions on how to get the most out of the sessions in this resource and how to use the accompanying resources on the Explore Together website (www.exploretogether.org).

Three more Explore Together resource books are also available, each with 12 sessions on a variety of themes.

The six steps

There are six essential steps to an Explore Together session, each of which can be tailored to slot into any existing structure and space:

1 **Prepare**
2 **Presenting the Bible**
3 **Pray**
4 **Explore**
5 **Share**
6 **Giving thanks**

These steps are explained in detail in each session outline.

Step 4 provides an opportunity for people to engage with God's Word using the Explore Together questions and the six Explore Together zones. Each zone has been carefully designed to cater for particular learning needs and preferences:

 Colour Zone –
for those who learn by seeing

 Listening Zone –
for those who learn by hearing

 Chat Zone –
for those who learn by thinking aloud

 Word Zone –
for those who learn by reading

 Busy Zone –
for those who learn by doing

 Quiet Zone –
for those who learn by reflecting

Individuals can choose to spend all of their exploring time in one zone, but may also choose to visit several zones, depending upon their preferences. There is no right or wrong amount of time to spend in a zone.

It is quite deliberate that no specific instructions are provided for each zone. Individuals are free to engage however they like with the resources provided in each area as they consider the Explore Together questions for the session.

Basic kit

Although every Explore Together session is different, there are some common elements that are always included. We will refer to these as the 'basic kit' for Explore Together. Before running your first session we advise that you acquire the following items, and top them up as required:

- Explore Together zone signs (available from www.exploretogether.org)
- Explore Together background soundtrack (available from www.exploretogether.org)
- MP3 players (or the means to play downloaded MP3 tracks – eg CDs and CD player)
- plasticine, play dough or clay
- plastic building bricks
- junk modelling items
- pipe cleaners
- pens, pencils and paper
- coloured pencils/pens
- coloured chalk sticks
- pastels/crayons
- glue
- scissors (child-safe)
- masking tape
- white paper
- black paper
- paper of different sorts, sizes and colours
- manuscript paper
- squared paper
- lined paper
- sticky notes
- a selection of Bible commentaries
- a selection of Bibles (different translations)
- children's Bibles and Bible story books, eg *The Big Bible Storybook* (Scripture Union, 2007)
- chairs/cushions/beanbags
- a separate area where people can be quiet

Each session will need a selection of other resources, detailed in Step 1. Many multimedia resources for each session are available for free from www.exploretogether.org/downloads (using the code from the bottom of page 32).

Gathering a team

Although it is entirely possible to lead an Explore Together session alone, it is much more effective when there is a team of people working together to share the responsibility and to model involvement. Strategically placed active participants will encourage others to participate.

The colour, word and busy zones benefit from having a carefully placed team member present to keep the focus on the questions, to engage in the zone activity and to draw people into the questions without dominating. The chat zone requires an experienced host to keep everyone focused.

For detailed team member role descriptions, visit www.exploretogether.org.

FAQs

If you have any further questions, it's likely we've answered them in our FAQ section on pages 30 and 31 at the back of this book. If not, please don't hesitate to get in touch via the Scripture Union website: www.scriptureunion.org.uk.

If you'd like to know more about the ideas that underpin Explore Together and hear about our experiences of Explore Together in action, please read our companion book:

Explore Together: The Journey

Joseph and his brothers

Genesis 37:1–11

Themes: God's plan, families, brothers, bullying, jealousy, dreams

Joseph and his coat of many colours is both a popular and familiar story to many, but there is always more that God wants to reveal to us through his Word. As you engage with this passage, ask God to show you something new!

When using this session you might choose to focus only on the suggested verses, or perhaps include an overview of the whole story.

Prepare

Resources required

- 'Joseph and his brothers' image collection
- 'Joseph and his brothers' word collection
- 'Joseph and his brothers' audio recording (from *The Big Bible Storybook* audio book)
- 'Joseph and his brothers' story text (from *The Big Bible Storybook*)
- Genesis 37:1–11 (CEV)
- 'Joseph and his brothers' Explore Together questions (PDF and PowerPoint)

All available from www.exploretogether.org/downloads (using the code from the bottom of page 32).

You will also need to gather:

- a roll of white paper
- paints, brushes and cover-up materials
- coloured tissue paper
- audio versions of different translations of Genesis 37:1–11
- newspapers for people to cut words from
- wooden blocks and sandpaper
- strands of embroidery thread in many colours
- items from the Explore Together basic kit (see page 5)
- someone who can give a talk that provides an overview of the whole of Joseph's story

Presenting the Bible

With the community gathered together, begin by sharing the words from Genesis 37:1–11. Consider carefully which version of the Bible you choose to read from.

Alternatively or in addition you may choose to act out the story using a group of volunteers. This passage easily lends itself to improvised drama – simply allocate people to be Joseph, the brothers and Israel (Jacob), and read the story aloud – encouraging your actors to play their parts according to what they hear.

Without being tempted to answer them, introduce the following questions to your community for them to consider:

- **What do you want to say to God about this story?**
- **Who, or what, are you jealous of? Why? What do you want to say to God about this?**
- **How do you feel about your own family?**
- **How does it feel to know you are part of God's family?**

Pray

Pray for and with your community, asking God to help you hear from him. This time of prayer can be creative, interactive, responsive, meditative or sung. It could also include Communion and intercession. Ensure that there is a place set aside where people can go if they feel that they need someone to pray with them specifically. Have a small team of people available to offer prayer if required. Prayer ministry should be available throughout an Explore Together session.

Explore

Read out your questions from Step 2 again or display them on a screen. Remind your community to consider these questions as they separate into their explore zones. Some may choose to consider all the questions while others may focus on just one. Some may completely ignore the questions and just open themselves up to God.

Invite your community to separate into small groups, around the zone(s) of their preference. Explain that individuals are welcome to spend as much or as little time in each zone as they wish, engaging at whatever level they feel comfortable. Depending upon where your quiet zone is located, you may wish to provide directions and remind people not to disturb one another when using this space.

Colour Zone
- a roll of white paper
- paints, brushes and cover-up materials
- coloured tissue paper
- glue
- 'Joseph and his brothers' image collection
- copies of the 'Joseph and his brothers' ET questions

Listening Zone
- 'Joseph and his brothers' audio recording (from *The Big Bible Storybook* audio book)
- audio versions of different translations of Genesis 37:1–11
- copies of the 'Joseph and his brothers' ET questions
- someone who can give a talk that provides an overview of the whole of Joseph's story

Chat Zone
- a separate area with chairs, cushions or beanbags
- a chat zone host who is willing to read the passage again and then lead a discussion around the questions
- copies of Genesis 37:1–11 (CEV) or Bibles
- copies of the 'Joseph and his brothers' ET questions

Word Zone
- pens and pencils
- scissors and glue
- newspapers
- biblical commentaries relating to Genesis 37:1–11
- 'Joseph and his brothers' story text
- other children's Bibles and Bible story books containing a version of Genesis 37:1–11
- 'Joseph and his brothers' word collection
- copies of Genesis 37:1–11 (CEV) or Bibles
- copies of the 'Joseph and his brothers' ET questions

Busy Zone
- building bricks
- wooden blocks and sandpaper
- strands of embroidery thread in many colours
- copies of the 'Joseph and his brothers' ET questions

Quiet Zone
- a separate area where people can be alone with their thoughts and God
- 'Joseph and his brothers' image collection (optional)
- copies of Genesis 37:1–11 (CEV) or Bibles
- copies of the 'Joseph and his brothers' ET questions

Share

As your time for exploring together draws to a close, invite your community to come back together into small groups of three to five. Suggest that they share their responses to the questions posed at the beginning.

Giving thanks

Invite the explorers to share their reflections with the wider community, drawing together their responses and noting any common themes that emerge. Conclude by reading Genesis 37:1–11 again (from the same Bible version used earlier). Then lead your community in a prayer, thanking God for all that he has revealed through this story. Alternatively, use the closing activity from the website. Encourage your community to continue their conversations about this story as they leave, and to take with them any artwork/writings/thoughts from the session.

The burning bush

Exodus 3:1–18

In many ways Moses wasn't a likely candidate for the leader of God's people on their journey out of Egypt. He was a 'sort-of-prince' turned murderer turned shepherd who had run away into the desert – but God had a plan! Moses encountered God in the burning bush and his life was never the same!

Prepare

Resources required
- 'God talks to Moses' story text (from *The Big Bible Storybook*)
- 'God talks to Moses' audio recording (from *The Big Bible Storybook* audio book)
- 'The burning bush' image collection
- 'The burning bush' word collection
- Exodus 3:1–18 (CEV)
- 'The burning bush' Explore Together questions (PDF and PowerPoint)

All available from www.exploretogether.org/downloads (using the code from the bottom of page 32).

You will also need to gather:
- a video of burning flames (either make your own, or search online)
- small flame shapes cut from red, orange and yellow paper
- empty matchboxes
- audio versions of different translations of Exodus 3:1–18
- dictionaries
- a collection of dry sticks or twigs
- candles and something to light them with (used safely, and supervised)
- items from the Explore Together basic kit (see page 5)

Presenting the Bible

With the community gathered together, begin by sharing the words from Exodus 3:1–18. Consider carefully which version of the Bible you choose to read from.

Alternatively or in addition you may choose to use a video of burning flames as a background to your reading.

Without being tempted to answer them, introduce the following questions to your community for them to consider:

- **If you had been there, how might you have reacted to the burning bush?**
- **What does this story teach you about God?**
- **What do you want to say to God today?**
- **How do you feel about God's holiness?**

Pray

Pray for and with your community, asking God to help you hear from him. This time of prayer can be creative, interactive, responsive, meditative or sung. It could also include Communion and intercession. Ensure that there is a place set aside where people can go if they feel that they need someone to pray with them specifically. Have a small team of people available to offer prayer if required. Prayer ministry should be available throughout an Explore Together session.

You might also choose to create your own burning bush as part of your prayer time by inviting everyone to contribute a small flame shape of red, orange or yellow paper to a pre-drawn bush outline. As you invite people to add their flame, you might like to use the following words:

'Moses met God in the burning bush. Bring your own flames forward now and add them to our bush, while asking God to meet with you today.'

Explore

Read out your questions from Step 2 again or display them on a screen. Remind your community to consider these questions as they separate into their explore zones. Some may choose to consider all the questions while others may focus on just one. Some may completely ignore the questions and just open themselves up to God.

Invite your community to separate into small groups, around the zone(s) of their preference. Explain that individuals are welcome to spend as much or as little time in each zone as they wish, engaging at whatever level they feel comfortable. Depending upon where your quiet zone is located, you may wish to provide directions and remind people not to disturb one another when using this space.

Colour Zone

- black paper
- glue
- red, orange and yellow chalks
- white chalks
- small flame shapes cut from red, orange and yellow paper
- empty matchboxes
- 'The burning bush' image collection
- copies of the 'The burning bush' ET questions

Listening Zone

- 'God talks to Moses' audio recording (from *The Big Bible Storybook* audio book)
- audio recordings of different translations of Exodus 3:1–18
- copies of the 'The burning bush' ET questions

Chat Zone

- a separate area with chairs, cushions or beanbags
- a chat zone host who is willing to read the passage again and then lead a discussion around the questions
- copies of Exodus 3:1–18 (CEV) or Bibles
- copies of the 'The burning bush' ET questions

Word Zone

- pens, pencils, paper
- small flame shapes cut from red, orange and yellow paper
- dictionaries
- biblical commentaries relating to Exodus 3:1–18
- 'The burning bush' word collection
- 'God talks to Moses' story text
- children's Bibles and Bible story books containing a version of Exodus 3:1–18
- copies of Exodus 3:1–18 (CEV) or Bibles
- copies of the 'The burning bush' ET questions

Busy Zone

- modelling clay or plasticine
- pens and pencils
- a collection of dry sticks or twigs
- small flame shapes cut from red, orange and yellow paper
- copies of the 'The burning bush' ET questions

Quiet Zone

- a separate area where people can be alone with their thoughts and God
- 'The burning bush' image collection (optional)
- copies of Exodus 3:1–18 (CEV) or Bibles
- copies of the 'The burning bush' ET questions

Share

As your time for exploring together draws to a close, invite your community to come back together into small groups of three to five. Suggest that they share their responses to the questions posed at the beginning.

Giving thanks

Invite the explorers to share their reflections with the wider community, drawing together their responses and noting any common themes that emerge. Conclude by reading Exodus 3:1–18 again (from the same Bible version used earlier). Then lead your community in a prayer, thanking God for all that he has revealed through this story. Encourage your community to continue their conversations about this story as they leave, and to take with them any artwork/writings/thoughts from the session.

Crying out to God
Psalm 86

Themes: prayer, crying out to God, trust, following, praise, teaching, questioning, discipleship

Sometimes it feels as if God isn't there. Psalm 86, written by David, reveals a man who is desperate for God to intervene and make his presence known. Yet, in his desperation, David doesn't lose faith: in fact he honours and praises God. In difficult times, do we always turn to prayer and praise?

Prepare

Resources required
- 'Where are you, God?' prayer
- 'Crying out to God' image collection
- 'Crying out to God' word collection
- Psalm 86 (CEV)
- 'Crying out to God' Explore Together questions (PDF and PowerPoint)

All available from www.exploretogether.org/downloads (using the code from the bottom of page 32).

You will also need to gather:
- colourful (appropriate) pages from magazines for collage
- recordings of some evocative classical music pieces, such as 'The Hebrides Overture' (Felix Mendelssohn) and 'The Lark Ascending' (Ralph Vaughan Williams)
- audio versions of different translations of Psalm 86
- a set of alphabet stamps and ink pads
- bowls of materials with different textures, for example: wood chippings, sand, gravel, water, cotton wool
- items from the Explore Together basic kit (see page 5)

Presenting the Bible

With the community gathered together, begin by sharing the words from Psalm 86. Consider carefully which version of the Bible you choose to read from.

Alternatively or in addition you may choose to divide your community into two halves, and invite one half to read the odd verses of the psalm aloud and the other half to read the even verses aloud.

Without being tempted to answer them, introduce the following questions to your community for them to consider:

- **How easy is it to trust in God?**
- **What do you want to say to God today?**
- **In what situation do you long to see God intervene?**
- **What might God want to teach you today?**

Pray

Pray for and with your community, asking God to help you hear from him. This time of prayer can be creative, interactive, responsive, meditative or sung. It could also include Communion and intercession. Ensure that there is a place set aside where people can go if they feel that they need someone to pray with them specifically. Have a small team of people available to offer prayer if required. Prayer ministry should be available throughout an Explore Together session.

You may like to use the 'Where are you, God?' prayer as part of this time. You could either read this out as a prayer led from the front, or you could encourage your community to respond with the parts in bold.

Explore

Read out your questions from Step 2 again or display them on a screen. Remind your community to consider these questions as they separate into their explore zones. Some may choose to consider all the questions while others may focus on just one. Some may completely ignore the questions and just open themselves up to God.

Invite your community to separate into small groups, around the zone(s) of their preference. Explain that individuals are welcome to spend as much or as little time in each zone as they wish, engaging at whatever level they feel comfortable. Depending upon where your quiet zone is located, you may wish to provide directions and remind people not to disturb one another when using this space.

Colour Zone
- black paper
- white paper
- coloured chalks
- glue
- colourful (appropriate) pages from magazines for collage
- 'Crying out to God' image collection
- copies of the 'Crying out to God' ET questions

Listening Zone
- audio recordings of some evocative classical music pieces, such as 'The Hebrides Overture' (Felix Mendelssohn) and 'The Lark Ascending' (Ralph Vaughan Williams)
- audio versions of different translations of Psalm 86
- copies of the 'Crying out to God' ET questions

Chat Zone
- a separate area with chairs, cushions or beanbags
- a chat zone host who is willing to read the passage again and then lead a discussion around the questions
- copies of Psalm 86 (CEV) or Bibles
- copies of the 'Crying out to God' ET questions

Word Zone

- pens, pencils, paper
- sticky notes
- a set of alphabet stamps and ink pads
- 'Crying out to God' word collection
- children's Bibles and Bible story books containing a version of Psalm 86
- copies of Psalm 86 (CEV) or Bibles
- copies of the 'Crying out to God' ET questions

Busy Zone
- building bricks
- wax crayons
- white paper
- bowls of materials with different textures, for example: wood chippings, sand, gravel, water, cotton wool
- copies of the 'Crying out to God' ET questions

Quiet Zone
- a separate area where people can be alone with their thoughts and God
- 'Crying out to God' image collection (optional)
- copies of Psalm 86 (CEV) or Bibles
- copies of the 'Crying out to God' ET questions

Share

As your time for exploring together draws to a close, invite your community to come back together into small groups of three to five. Suggest that they share their responses to the questions posed at the beginning.

Giving thanks

Invite the explorers to share their reflections with the wider community, drawing together their responses and noting any common themes that emerge. Conclude by reading Psalm 86 again (from the same Bible version used earlier). Then lead your community in a prayer, thanking God for all that he has revealed through this story. Encourage your community to continue their conversations about this story as they leave, and to take with them any artwork/writings/thoughts from the session.

Praise the Lord

Psalm 150

God is always worthy of our praise and worship. Psalm 150 offers reasons to worship our almighty Father, and encourages us to praise him using music and song. But we all know you don't have to be a musician to praise God – how will you worship him today?

Prepare

Resources required
- 'Praise God' story text (from *The Big Bible Storybook*)
- 'Praise God' audio recording (from *The Big Bible Storybook* audio book)
- 'Praise the Lord' image collection
- 'Praise the Lord' word collection
- Psalm 150 (CEV)
- 'Praise the Lord' Explore Together questions (PDF and PowerPoint)

All available from www.exploretogether.org/downloads (using the code from the bottom of page 32).

You will also need to gather:
- a selection of easy-to-play musical instruments
- coloured matchsticks
- finger paints
- wet wipes
- audio versions of different translations of Psalm 150
- notebooks
- modelling clay and tools
- items from the Explore Together basic kit (see page 5)

Presenting the Bible

With the community gathered together, begin by sharing the words from Psalm 150. Consider carefully which version of the Bible you choose to read from.

Without being tempted to answer them, introduce the following questions to your community for them to consider:

- **What do you want to say to God today?**
- **What might God want to say to you?**
- **What do you want to praise God for?**
- **How might you worship God in a new way?**

Pray

Pray for and with your community, asking God to help you hear from him. This time of prayer can be creative, interactive, responsive, meditative or sung. It could also include communion and intercession. Ensure that there is a place set aside where people can go if they feel that they need someone to pray with them specifically. Have a small team of people available to offer prayer if required. Prayer ministry should be available throughout an Explore Together session.

You might choose to provide the instruments listed (or similar!) from Psalm 150 for your community, and use them to share in a time of prayer and worship together.

Explore

Read out your questions from Step 2 again or display them on a screen. Remind your community to consider these questions as they separate into their explore zones. Some may choose to consider all the questions while others may focus on just one. Some may completely ignore the questions and just open themselves up to God.

Invite your community to separate into small groups, around the zone(s) of their preference. Explain that individuals are welcome to spend as much or as little time in each zone as they wish, engaging at whatever level they feel comfortable. Depending upon where your quiet zone is located, you may wish to provide directions and remind people not to disturb one another when using this space.

Colour Zone
- coloured matchsticks
- glue
- black paper
- white paper
- finger paints
- wet wipes
- 'Praise the Lord' image collection
- copies of the 'Praise the Lord' ET questions

Listening Zone
- 'Praise God' audio recording (from *The Big Bible* Storybook audio book)
- audio versions of different translations of Psalm 150
- copies of the 'Praise the Lord' ET questions

Chat Zone
- a separate area with chairs, cushions or beanbags
- a chat zone host who is willing to read the passage again and then lead a discussion around the questions
- copies of Psalm 150 (CEV) or Bibles
- copies of the 'Praise the Lord' ET questions

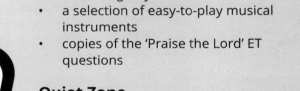

Word Zone
- pens, pencils, paper
- notebooks
- manuscript paper
- biblical commentaries relating to Psalm 150
- 'Praise the Lord' word collection
- 'Praise God' story text
- other children's Bibles and Bible story books containing a version of Psalm 150
- copies of Psalm 150 (CEV) or Bibles
- copies of the 'Praise the Lord' ET questions

Busy Zone
- building bricks
- modelling clay and tools
- a selection of easy-to-play musical instruments
- copies of the 'Praise the Lord' ET questions

Quiet Zone
- a separate area where people can be alone with their thoughts and God
- 'Praise the Lord' image collection (optional)
- copies of Psalm 150 (CEV) or Bibles
- copies of the 'Praise the Lord' ET questions

Share

As your time for exploring together draws to a close, invite your community to come back together into small groups of three to five. Suggest that they share their responses to the questions posed at the beginning.

Giving thanks

Invite the explorers to share their reflections with the wider community, drawing together their responses and noting any common themes that emerge. Conclude by reading Psalm 150 again (from the same Bible version used earlier). Then lead your community in a prayer, thanking God for all that he has revealed through this story. Encourage your community to continue their conversations about this story as they leave, and to take with them any artwork/writings/thoughts from the session.

All who are thirsty

Isaiah 55:1–12

Themes: God's provision, trust, weakness, water, following God, joy, hope

Isaiah knows that only God can meet his real needs. Trusting in God can bring great joy and hope, but that doesn't mean it's easy to do! How can you learn to depend on God and seek him first in times of need?

Prepare

Resources required

- 'All who are thirsty' image collection
- 'All who are thirsty' word collection
- Isaiah 55:1–12 (CEV)
- 'All who are thirsty' Explore Together questions (PDF and PowerPoint)

All available from www.exploretogether.org/downloads (using the code from the bottom of page 32).

You will also need to gather:

- paints, brushes and cover-up materials
- jugs of water and plastic cups
- audio versions of different translations of Psalm 150
- audio versions of 'All who are thirsty' (Brenton Brown, © Copyright 1998 Vineyard Songs)
- large pieces of coloured fabric
- palm-sized smooth pebbles
- a small, indoor water feature (optional)
- items from the Explore Together basic kit (see page 5)

Presenting the Bible

With the community gathered together, begin by sharing the words from Isaiah 55:1–12. Consider carefully which version of the Bible you choose to read from.

In addition you may choose to use the following song as part of this time:

- 'All who are thirsty' (Brenton Brown, © Copyright 1998 Vineyard Songs)

Without being tempted to answer them, introduce the following questions to your community for them to consider:

- **Why does God want you to hear this message today?**
- **In what ways does God meet your needs?**
- **What does God want to give you today?**
- **What do you want to say to God?**

Pray

Pray for and with your community, asking God to help you hear from him. This time of prayer can be creative, interactive, responsive, meditative or sung. It could also include Communion and intercession. Ensure that there is a place set aside where people can go if they feel that they need someone to pray with them specifically. Have a small team of people available to offer prayer if required. Prayer ministry should be available throughout an Explore Together session.

Explore

Read out your questions from Step 2 again or display them on a screen. Remind your community to consider these questions as they separate into their explore zones. Some may choose to consider all the questions while others may focus on just one. Some may completely ignore the questions and just open themselves up to God.

Invite your community to separate into small groups, around the zone(s) of their preference. Explain that individuals are welcome to spend as much or as little time in each zone as they wish, engaging at whatever level they feel comfortable. Depending upon where your quiet zone is located, you may wish to provide directions and remind people not to disturb one another when using this space.

Colour Zone
* white paper
* coloured paper
* scissors
* glue
* 'All who are thirsty' image collection
* paints, brushes and cover-up materials
* jugs of water and plastic cups
* copies of the 'All who are thirsty' ET questions

Listening Zone
* audio versions of different translations of Isaiah 55:1–12
* audio versions of 'All who are thirsty' (Brenton Brown, © Copyright 1998 Vineyard Songs)
* jugs of water and plastic cups
* copies of the 'All who are thirsty' ET questions

Chat Zone

* a separate area with chairs, cushions or beanbags
* a chat zone host who is willing to read the passage again and then lead a discussion around the questions
* jugs of water and plastic cups
* copies of Isaiah 55:1–12 (CEV) or Bibles
* copies of the 'All who are thirsty' ET questions

Word Zone
* pens, pencils, paper
* biblical commentaries relating to Isaiah 55:1–12
* 'All who are thirsty' word collection
* children's Bibles and Bible story books containing a version of Isaiah 55:1–12
* copies of Isaiah 55:1–12 (CEV) or Bibles
* jugs of water and plastic cups
* copies of the 'All who are thirsty' ET questions

Busy Zone
* building bricks
* large pieces of coloured fabric
* palm-sized smooth pebbles
* a small, indoor water feature (optional)
* jugs of water and plastic cups
* copies of the 'All who are thirsty' ET questions

Quiet Zone

* a separate area where people can be alone with their thoughts and God
* jugs of water and plastic cups
* 'All who are thirsty' image collection (optional)
* copies of Isaiah 55:1–12 (CEV) or Bibles
* copies of the 'All who are thirsty' ET questions

Share

As your time for exploring together draws to a close, invite your community to come back together into small groups of three to five. Suggest that they share their responses to the questions posed at the beginning.

Giving thanks

Invite the explorers to share their reflections with the wider community, drawing together their responses and noting any common themes that emerge. Conclude by reading Isaiah 55:1–12 again (from the same Bible version used earlier). Then lead your community in a prayer, thanking God for all that he has revealed through this story. Encourage your community to continue their conversations about this story as they leave, and to take with them any artwork/writings/thoughts from the session.

Good Friday
John 19:1–30

This session is designed to help your community explore the events of Good Friday in a way that is meaningful to them. It can be used indoors or outdoors (with a little adaptation), and with people of all ages and stages of faith.

Prepare

Resources required
- 'Jesus dies' audio recording (from *The Big Bible Storybook* audio book)
- 'Good Friday' monologue
- 'Good Friday' image collection
- 'Good Friday' word collection
- John 19:1–30 (CEV)
- 'Good Friday' Explore Together questions (PDF and PowerPoint)

All available from www.exploretogether.org/downloads (using the code from the bottom of page 32).

You will also need to gather:
- a roll of white paper
- black marker pens
- hot cross buns
- audio versions of different translations of John 19:1–30
- lined notebooks
- items from the Explore Together basic kit (see page 5)
- someone to deliver a Good Friday themed talk

Presenting the Bible

With the community gathered together, begin by sharing the words from John 19:1–30. Consider carefully which version of the Bible you choose to read from.

Without being tempted to answer them, introduce the following questions to your community for them to consider:

- **How do you feel about what happened to Jesus?**
- **What would you like to say to Jesus today?**
- **How does it feel to know that Jesus died for you?**
- **What does God's love mean to you?**

Pray

Pray for and with your community, asking God to help you hear from him. This time of prayer can be creative, interactive, responsive, meditative or sung. It could also include Communion and intercession. Ensure that there is a place set aside where people can go if they feel that they need someone to pray with them specifically. Have a small team of people available to offer prayer if required. Prayer ministry should be available throughout an Explore Together session.

Explore

Read out your questions from Step 2 again or display them on a screen. Remind your community to consider these questions as they separate into their explore zones. Some may choose to consider all the questions while others may focus on just one. Some may completely ignore the questions and just open themselves up to God.

Invite your community to separate into small groups, around the zone(s) of their preference. Explain that individuals are welcome to spend as much or as little time in each zone as they wish, engaging at whatever level they feel comfortable. Depending upon where your quiet zone is located, you may wish to provide directions and remind people not to disturb one another when using this space.

Colour Zone
- black paper
- coloured pastels
- white chalk
- a roll of white paper
- black marker pens
- hot cross buns
- 'Good Friday' image collection
- copies of the 'Good Friday' ET questions

Listening Zone
- 'Jesus dies' audio recording (from *The Big Bible Storybook* audio book)
- audio versions of different translations of John 19:1–30
- hot cross buns
- copies of the 'Good Friday' ET questions
- someone to deliver a Good Friday themed talk

Chat Zone
- a separate area with chairs, cushions or beanbags
- a chat zone host who is willing to read the passage again and then lead a discussion around the questions
- hot cross buns
- copies of John 19:1–30 (CEV) or Bibles
- copies of the 'Good Friday' ET questions

Word Zone

- lined notebooks
- sticky notes
- copies of the 'Good Friday' monologue
- pens, pencils, paper
- biblical commentaries relating to John 19:1–30
- 'Good Friday' word collection
- hot cross buns
- copies of *The Big Bible Storybook* open at 'Jesus dies', or other children's Bibles and Bible story books containing a version of John 19:1–30
- copies of John 19:1–30 (CEV) or Bibles
- copies of the 'Good Friday' ET questions

Busy Zone
- modelling clay
- building blocks
- hot cross buns
- copies of the 'Good Friday' ET questions

Quiet Zone
- a separate area where people can be alone with their thoughts and God
- 'Good Friday' image collection (optional)
- hot cross buns
- copies of John 19:1–30 (CEV) or Bibles
- copies of the 'Good Friday' ET questions

Share

As your time for exploring together draws to a close, invite your community to come back together into small groups of three to five. Suggest that they share their responses to the questions posed at the beginning.

Giving thanks

Invite the explorers to share their reflections with the wider community, drawing together their responses and noting any common themes that emerge. Conclude by reading John 19:1–30 again (from the same Bible version used earlier). Then lead your community in a prayer, thanking God for all that he has revealed through this story. Encourage your community to continue their conversations about this story as they leave, and to take with them any artwork/writings/thoughts from the session.

The widow's son
Luke 7:11–17

As Jesus and his disciples approached Nain, they met a widow and her dead son, along with a large crowd of neighbours. And Jesus felt compassion. The miracle that followed caused the people to fear and praise God, and to spread news of Jesus widely.

Prepare

Resources required
- 'Jesus helps a woman' story text (from *The Big BibleStorybook*)
- 'Jesus helps a woman' audio recording (from *The Big Bible Storybook* audio book)
- 'The widow's son' word collection
- 'The widow's son' image collection
- Luke 7:11–17 (CEV)
- 'The widow's son' Explore Together questions (PDF and PowerPoint)

All available from www.exploretogether.org/downloads (using the code from the bottom of page 32).

You will also need to gather:
- flags and ribbons
- audio versions of different translations of Luke 7:11–17
- fabric and drinking straws
- items from the Explore Together basic kit (see page 5)
- someone to deliver a short sermon on Luke 7:11–17 (optional)

Presenting the Bible

With the community gathered together, begin by sharing the words from Luke 7:11–17. Consider carefully which version of the Bible you choose to read from.

Without being tempted to answer them, introduce the following questions to your community for them to consider:

- **When or how have you 'seen the hand of God at work'?**
- **Where would you place yourself in this miraculous account of events?**
- **How do your encounters with God impact your work, family, community and further afield?**

Pray

Pray for and with your community, asking God to help you hear from him. This time of prayer can be creative, interactive, responsive, meditative or sung. It could also include Communion and intercession. Ensure that there is a place set aside where people can go if they feel that they need someone to pray with them specifically. Have a small team of people available to offer prayer if required. Prayer ministry should be available throughout an Explore Together session.

Explore

Read out your questions from Step 2 again or display them on a screen. Remind your community to consider these questions as they separate into their explore zones. Some may choose to consider all the questions while others may focus on just one. Some may completely ignore the questions and just open themselves up to God.

Invite your community to separate into small groups, around the zone(s) of their preference. Explain that individuals are welcome to spend as much or as little time in each zone as they wish, engaging at whatever level they feel comfortable. Depending upon where your quiet zone is located, you may wish to provide directions and remind people not to disturb one another when using this space.

Colour Zone
- crayons, coloured pencils and pens
- black paper
- flags and ribbons
- 'The widow's son' image collection
- copies of the 'The widow's son' ET questions

Listening Zone
- 'Jesus helps a woman' audio recording (from *The Big Bible Storybook* audio book)
- audio versions of different translations of Luke 7:11–17
- copies of the 'The widow's son' ET questions
- you may wish to deliver a short sermon in this zone

Chat Zone
- a separate area with chairs, cushions or beanbags
- a chat zone host who is willing to read the passage again and then lead a discussion around the questions
- copies of Luke 7:11–17 (CEV) or Bibles
- copies of the 'The widow's son' ET questions

Word Zone

- pens, pencils, paper
- biblical commentaries relating to Luke 7:11–17
- 'Jesus helps a woman' story text (from *The Big Bible Storybook*)
- other children's Bibles and Bible story books containing a version of Luke 7:11–17
- copies of Luke 7:11–17 (CEV) or Bibles
- 'The widow's son' word collection
- copies of the 'The widow's son' ET questions

Busy Zone
- plasticine, play dough or clay
- pipe cleaners
- fabric and drinking straws
- copies of the 'The widow's son' ET questions

Quiet Zone

- a separate area where people can be alone with their thoughts and God
- 'The widow's son' image collection (optional)
- copies of Luke 7:11–17 (CEV) or Bibles
- copies of the 'The widow's son' ET questions

Share

As your time for exploring together draws to a close, invite your community to come back together into small groups of three to five. Suggest that they share their responses to the questions posed at the beginning.

Giving thanks

Invite the explorers to share their reflections with the wider community, drawing together their responses and noting any common themes that emerge. Conclude by reading Luke 7:11–17 again (from the same Bible version used earlier). Then lead your community in a prayer, thanking God for all that he has revealed through this story. Encourage your community to continue their conversations about this story as they leave, and to take with them any artwork/writings/thoughts from the session.

Sending 72
Luke 10:1–20

Themes: equip, trust, workers, kingdom, power, heaven

When Jesus sent out the 72, he did not provide for them. He offered them a glimpse of the difficulty and sacrifice involved with following him, but also the joy. They returned excited!

Prepare

Resources required
- 'Sending 72' image collection
- 'Sending 72' word collection
- Luke 10:1–20 (CEV)
- 'Sending 72' Explore Together questions (PDF and PowerPoint)

All available from www.exploretogether.org/downloads (using the code from the bottom of page 32).

You will also need to gather:
- Scratch Art doodle sheets
- audio versions of different translations of Luke 10:1–20
- lined notebooks
- beads and thread
- items from the Explore Together basic kit (see page 5)
- someone to deliver a short talk about Luke 10:1–20, using the suggested teaching outline, if desired (optional)

Presenting the Bible

With the community gathered together, begin by sharing the words from Luke 10:1–20. Consider carefully which version of the Bible you choose to read from.

Without being tempted to answer them, introduce the following questions to your community for them to consider:

- **How has God used you to share his love and story?**
- **Where or to whom is God sending you to share his love and story?**
- **Who has God given to support you as you do this?**

Pray

Pray for and with your community, asking God to help you hear from him. This time of prayer can be creative, interactive, responsive, meditative or sung. It could also include Communion and intercession. Ensure that there is a place set aside where people can go if they feel that they need someone to pray with them specifically. Have a small team of people available to offer prayer if required. Prayer ministry should be available throughout an Explore Together session.

Explore

Read out your questions from Step 2 again or display them on a screen. Remind your community to consider these questions as they separate into their explore zones. Some may choose to consider all the questions while others may focus on just one. Some may completely ignore the questions and just open themselves up to God.

Invite your community to separate into small groups, around the zone(s) of their preference. Explain that individuals are welcome to spend as much or as little time in each zone as they wish, engaging at whatever level they feel comfortable. Depending upon where your quiet zone is located, you may wish to provide directions and remind people not to disturb one another when using this space.

Colour Zone
- coloured chalk sticks, glue and black paper
- coloured pastels, crayons and white paper
- Scratch Art doodle sheets
- 'Sending 72' image collection
- copies of the 'Sending 72' ET questions

Listening Zone
- audio versions of different translations of Luke 10:1–20
- copies of the 'Sending 72' ET questions
- you may wish to deliver a short talk in this zone

Chat Zone
- a separate area with chairs, cushions or beanbags
- a chat zone host who is willing to read the passage again and then lead a discussion around the questions
- copies of Luke 10:1–20 (CEV) or Bibles
- copies of the 'Sending 72' ET questions

Word Zone

- lined notebooks
- pens, pencils
- biblical commentaries relating to Luke 10:1–20
- 'Sending 72' word collection
- children's Bibles and Bible story books containing a version of Luke 10:1–20
- copies of Luke 10:1–20 (CEV) or Bibles
- copies of the 'Sending 72' ET questions

Busy Zone

- junk modelling items
- plastic building bricks
- beads and thread
- copies of the 'Sending 72' ET questions

Quiet Zone
- a separate area where people can be alone with their thoughts and God
- 'Sending 72' image collection (optional)
- copies of Luke 10:1–20 (CEV) or Bibles
- copies of the 'Sending 72' ET questions

Share

As your time for exploring together draws to a close, invite your community to come back together into small groups of three to five. Suggest that they share their responses to the questions posed at the beginning.

Giving thanks

Invite the explorers to share their reflections with the wider community, drawing together their responses and noting any common themes that emerge. Conclude by reading Luke 10:1–20 again (from the same Bible version used earlier). Then lead your community in a prayer, thanking God for all that he has revealed through this story. Encourage your community to continue their conversations about this story as they leave, and to take with them any artwork/writings/thoughts from the session.

The first disciples
John 1:35–51

Jesus chose a group of very different people to be his followers, and revealed himself to them indifferent ways. Look around the group gathered today and thank God for the range of people called to his service.

Prepare

Resources required
- 'Jesus the leader' story text (from *The Big Bible Storybook*)
- 'Jesus the leader' audio recording (from *The Big Bible Storybook* audio book)
- person outline
- 'The first disciples' word collection
- 'The first disciples' image collection
- John 1:35–51 (CEV)
- 'The first disciples' Explore Together questions (PDF and PowerPoint)

All available from www.exploretogether.org/downloads (using the code from the bottom of page 32).

You will also need to gather:
- colourful pictures of people from magazines
- audio versions of different translations of John 1:35–51
- items from the Explore Together basic kit (see page 5)

Presenting the Bible

With the community gathered together, begin by sharing the words from John 1:35–51. Consider carefully which version of the Bible you choose to read from.

Without being tempted to answer them, introduce the following questions to your community for them to consider:

- **What part does God want you to play?**
- **Why does God want you to be part of his plan?**
- **What do you want to say to God?**

Pray

Pray for and with your community, asking God to help you hear from him. This time of prayer can be creative, interactive, responsive, meditative or sung. It could also include Communion and intercession. Ensure that there is a place set aside where people can go if they feel that they need someone to pray with them specifically. Have a small team of people available to offer prayer if required. Prayer ministry should be available throughout an Explore Together session.

Explore

Read out your questions from Step 2 again or display them on a screen. Remind your community to consider these questions as they separate into their explore zones. Some may choose to consider all the questions while others may focus on just one. Some may completely ignore the questions and just open themselves up to God.

Invite your community to separate into small groups, around the zone(s) of their preference. Explain that individuals are welcome to spend as much or as little time in each zone as they wish, engaging at whatever level they feel comfortable. Depending upon where your quiet zone is located, you may wish to provide directions and remind people not to disturb one another when using this space.

Colour Zone
- coloured chalk sticks
- green, black and white paper
- colourful pictures of people from magazines
- glue
- 'The first disciples' image collection
- copies of the 'The first disciples' ET questions

Listening Zone
- 'Jesus the leader' audio recording (from *The Big Bible Storybook* audio book)
- audio versions of different translations of John 1:35–51
- copies of the 'The first disciples' ET questions

Chat Zone
- a separate area with chairs, cushions or beanbags
- a chat zone host who is willing to read the passage again and then lead a discussion around the questions
- copies of John 1:35–51 (CEV) or Bibles
- copies of the 'The first disciples' ET questions

Word Zone

- pens, pencils
- plain paper of different sizes, ruled and squared paper
- biblical commentaries relating to John 1:35–51
- 'Jesus the leader' story text (from *The Big Bible Storybook*)
- children's Bibles and Bible story books containing a version of John 1:35–51
- copies of John 1:35–51 (CEV) or Bibles
- 'The first disciples' word collection
- copies of the 'The first disciples' ET questions

Busy Zone
- plastic building bricks
- junk modelling items
- pipe cleaners
- copies of person outline
- copies of the 'The first disciples' ET questions

Quiet Zone

- a separate area where people can be alone with their thoughts and God
- 'The first disciples' image collection (optional)
- copies of John 1:35–51 (CEV) or Bibles
- copies of the 'The first disciples' ET questions

Share

As your time for exploring together draws to a close, invite your community to come back together into small groups of three to five. Suggest that they share their responses to the questions posed at the beginning.

Giving thanks

Invite the explorers to share their reflections with the wider community, drawing together their responses and noting any common themes that emerge. Conclude by reading John 1:35–51 again (from the same Bible version used earlier). Then lead your community in a prayer, thanking God for all that he has revealed through this story. Encourage your community to continue their conversations about this story as they leave, and to take with them any artwork/writings/thoughts from the session.

Spiritual gifts
1 Corinthians 12:1–11

Before he lists some of the spiritual gifts, Paul reminds his readers that they are all led by God's Spirit and that there are different ways of serving. He encourages them to remember that God works in the life of all believers, helping them in all they do.

Prepare

Resources required
- 'Old Testament miracles' passages list
- 'Miracles of Jesus' passages list
- 'Spiritual gifts' image collection
- 'Spiritual gifts' word collection
- 1 Corinthians 12:1–11 (CEV)
- 'Spiritual gifts' Explore Together questions

All available from www.exploretogether.org/downloads (using the code from the bottom of page 32).

You will also need to gather:
- paints and brushes
- ribbons and flags of various colours and lengths
- audio versions of different translations of 1 Corinthians 12:1–11
- items from the Explore Together basic kit (see page 5)
- someone to deliver a short talk on 1 Corinthians 12:1–11 (optional)

Presenting the Bible

With the community gathered together, begin by sharing the words from 1 Corinthians 12:1–11. Consider carefully which version of the Bible you choose to read from.

Without being tempted to answer them, introduce the following questions to your community for them to consider:

- **Why does God give us gifts?**
- **Which gifts would you like to have?**
- **Which gifts would you not like to have?**
- **What does God want you to say to him?**

Pray

Pray for and with your community, asking God to help you hear from him. This time of prayer can be creative, interactive, responsive, meditative or sung. It could also include communion and intercession. Ensure that there is a place set aside where people can go if they feel that they need someone to pray with them specifically. Have a small team of people available to offer prayer if required. Prayer ministry should be available throughout an Explore Together session.

Explore

Read out your questions from Step 2 again or display them on a screen. Remind your community to consider these questions as they separate into their explore zones. Some may choose to consider all the questions while others may focus on just one. Some may completely ignore the questions and just open themselves up to God.

Invite your community to separate into small groups, around the zone(s) of their preference. Explain that individuals are welcome to spend as much or as little time in each zone as they wish, engaging at whatever level they feel comfortable. Depending upon where your quiet zone is located, you may wish to provide directions and remind people not to disturb one another when using this space.

Colour Zone
- paint, brushes, paper
- coloured pastels, crayons and white paper
- flags and ribbons of different colours and lengths, for dancing/moving with
- 'Spiritual gifts' image collection
- copies of the 'Spiritual gifts' ET questions

Listening Zone
- audio versions of different translations of 1 Corinthians 12:1–11
- copies of the 'Spiritual gifts' ET questions
- a talk or sermon based on this passage could be shared

Chat Zone
- a separate area with chairs, cushions or beanbags
- a chat zone host who is willing to read the passage again and then lead a discussion around the questions
- copies of 1 Corinthians 12:1–11 (CEV) or Bibles
- copies of the 'Spiritual gifts' ET questions

Word Zone

- pens, pencils
- sticky notes
- biblical commentaries relating to 1 Corinthians 12:1–11
- 'Spiritual gifts' word collection
- children's Bibles and Bible story books containing a version of 1 Corinthians 12:1–11
- copies of 1 Corinthians 12:1–11 (CEV) or Bibles
- copies of the 'Spiritual gifts' ET questions

Busy Zone

- small boxes
- coloured wrapping paper
- sticky tape
- plastic building bricks
- scissors, glue
- copies of the 'Spiritual gifts' ET questions

Quiet Zone
- a separate area where people can be alone with their thoughts and God
- 'Spiritual gifts' image collection (optional)
- copies of 1 Corinthians 12:1–11 (CEV) or Bibles
- copies of the 'Spiritual gifts' ET questions

Share

As your time for exploring together draws to a close, invite your community to come back together into small groups of three to five. Suggest that they share their responses to the questions posed at the beginning.

Giving thanks

Invite the explorers to share their reflections with the wider community, drawing together their responses and noting any common themes that emerge. Conclude by reading 1 Corinthians 12:1–11 again (from the same Bible version used earlier). Then lead your community in a prayer, thanking God for all that he has revealed through this story. Encourage your community to continue their conversations about this story as they leave, and to take with them any artwork/writings/thoughts from the session.

What is love?

1 Corinthians 13

Themes: love, patience, kindness, commitment, faithfulness, forgiveness, hope

This session provides space for your community to consider God's love for them, their love for God and their expressions of love for others.

Prepare

Resources required
- 'What is love?' image collection
- 'What is love?' word collection
- 'How do I love?' poem
- 1 Corinthians 13 (CEV)
- 'What is love?' Explore Together questions (PDF and PowerPoint)

All available from www.exploretogether.org/downloads (using the code from the bottom of page 32).

You will also need to gather:
- 'Love Is Patient and Kind' video by Logos Bible Software, available on YouTube at: www.youtube.com/watch?v=8F9_A7XIU6k
- coloured tissue paper
- heart shapes of various sizes cut from different coloured paper
- audio versions of different translations of 1 Corinthians 13
- shallow trays with play sand inside for drawing in
- items from the Explore Together basic kit (see page 5)
- someone to deliver a sermon on 1 Corinthians 13

Presenting the Bible

With the community gathered together, begin by sharing the words from 1 Corinthians 13. Consider carefully which version of the Bible you choose to read from.

Alternatively or in addition you may choose to use the following:
- 'Love Is Patient and Kind' video by Logos Bible Software, available on YouTube at: www.youtube.com/watch?v=8F9_A7XIU6k

Without being tempted to answer them, introduce the following questions to your community for them to consider:

- **How do you feel about God's love for you?**
- **Are you loving others as well as you can?**
- **Who do you know that needs to feel God's love?**
- **What do you want to say to God today?**

Pray

Pray for and with your community, asking God to help you hear from him. This time of prayer can be creative, interactive, responsive, meditative or sung. It could also include Communion and intercession. Ensure that there is a place set aside where people can go if they feel that they need someone to pray with them specifically. Have a small team of people available to offer prayer if required. Prayer ministry should be available throughout an Explore Together session.

You might like to invite your community to take a moment in silence to consider God's unconditional love for them.

Explore

Read out your questions from Step 2 again or display them on a screen. Remind your community to consider these questions as they separate into their explore zones. Some may choose to consider all the questions while others may focus on just one. Some may completely ignore the questions and just open themselves up to God.

Invite your community to separate into small groups, around the zone(s) of their preference. Explain that individuals are welcome to spend as much or as little time in each zone as they wish, engaging at whatever level they feel comfortable. Depending upon where your quiet zone is located, you may wish to provide directions and remind people not to disturb one another when using this space.

Colour Zone
- coloured pencils
- pastels
- white paper
- glue
- 'What is love?' image collection
- coloured tissue paper
- heart shapes of various sizes cut from different coloured paper
- copies of the 'What is love?' ET questions

Listening Zone
- audio versions of different translations of 1 Corinthians 13
- copies of the 'What is love?' ET questions
- someone to deliver a sermon on 1 Corinthians 13

Chat Zone
- a separate area with chairs, cushions or beanbags
- a chat zone host who is willing to read the passage again and then lead a discussion around the questions
- ccopies of 1 Corinthians 13 (CEV) or Bibles
- copies of the 'What is love?' ET questions

Word Zone

- pens, pencils, paper
- sticky notes
- biblical commentaries relating to 1 Corinthians 13
- 'What is love?' word collection
- 'How do I love?' poem
- Bible story books containing a version of 1 Corinthians 13
- copies of 1 Corinthians 13 (CEV) or Bibles
- copies of the 'What is love?' ET questions

Busy Zone

- black paper
- white chalk
- items for junk modelling
- shallow trays with play sand inside for drawing in
- copies of the 'What is love?' ET questions

Quiet Zone

- a separate area where people can be alone with their thoughts and God
- 'What is love?' image collection (optional)
- 'What is love?' word collection (optional)
- copies of 1 Corinthians 13 (CEV) or Bibles
- copies of the 'What is love?' ET questions

Share

As your time for exploring together draws to a close, invite your community to come back together into small groups of three to five. Suggest that they share their responses to the questions posed at the beginning.

Giving thanks

Invite the explorers to share their reflections with the wider community, drawing together their responses and noting any common themes that emerge. Conclude by reading 1 Corinthians 13 again (from the same Bible version used earlier). Then lead your community in a prayer, thanking God for all that he has revealed through this story. Encourage your community to continue their conversations about this story as they leave, and to take with them any artwork/writings/thoughts from the session.

There will be a day

Revelation 21:1–4

Themes: heaven, hope, justice, freedom, God's promises, judgement, eternal life, restoration

Knowing that one day God will make all things well, that he will bring an end to all pain and suffering is a wonderful source of hope. But what does this promise of a glorious future mean for us here and now?

Prepare

Resources required
- 'The City of God' audio recording (from *The Big Bible Storybook* audio book)
- 'There will be a day' image collection
- 'There will be a day' word collection
- Revelation 21:1–4 (CEV)
- 'There will be a day' Explore Together questions (PDF and PowerPoint)

All available from www.exploretogether.org/downloads (using the code from the bottom of page 32).

You will also need to gather:
- audio versions of 'There will be a day' (Jeremy Camp, © 2008 BEC Recordings) (optional)
- audio versions of 'There is a day' (Phatfish, © 2013 Phatmusic) (optional)
- gold and silver paper
- gold and silver pens
- sticking plasters
- items from the Explore Together basic kit (see page 5)

Presenting the Bible

With the community gathered together, begin by sharing the words from Revelation 21:1–4. Consider carefully which version of the Bible you choose to read from.

In addition you may choose to use the following song(s) as part of this time.

- 'There will be a day' (Jeremy Camp, © 2008 BEC Recordings)
- 'There is a day' (Phatfish, © 2013 Phatmusic)

Without being tempted to answer them, introduce the following questions to your community for them to consider:

- **What might God want to say to you today?**
- **What do you want to say to God?**
- **How do you feel about the new heaven and the new earth described in this passage?**
- **How might this passage motivate you to live differently today?**

Pray

Pray for and with your community, asking God to help you hear from him. This time of prayer can be creative, interactive, responsive, meditative or sung. It could also include Communion and intercession. Ensure that there is a place set aside where people can go if they feel that they need someone to pray with them specifically. Have a small team of people available to offer prayer if required. Prayer ministry should be available throughout an Explore Together session.

Explore

Read out your questions from Step 2 again or display them on a screen. Remind your community to consider these questions as they separate into their explore zones. Some may choose to consider all the questions while others may focus on just one. Some may completely ignore the questions and just open themselves up to God.

Invite your community to separate into small groups, around the zone(s) of their preference. Explain that individuals are welcome to spend as much or as little time in each zone as they wish, engaging at whatever level they feel comfortable. Depending upon where your quiet zone is located, you may wish to provide directions and remind people not to disturb one another when using this space.

Colour Zone
- white paper
- black paper
- coloured chalks and pastels
- scissors, glue
- gold and silver paper
- gold and silver pens
- 'There will be a day' image collection
- copies of the 'There will be a day' ET questions

Listening Zone
- 'The City of God' audio recording (from *The Big Bible Storybook* audio book)
- audio versions of different translations of Revelation 21:1–4
- audio versions of 'There will be a day' (Jeremy Camp; © 2008 BEC Recordings) (optional)
- audio versions of 'There is a day' (Phatfish; © 2013 Phatmusic) (optional)
- copies of the 'There will be a day' ET questions

Chat Zone
- a separate area with chairs, cushions or beanbags
- a chat zone host who is willing to read the passage again and then lead a discussion around the questions
- copies of Revelation 21:1–4 (CEV) or Bibles
- copies of the 'There will be a day' ET questions

Word Zone
- pens, pencils, paper
- sticky notes
- biblical commentaries relating to Revelation 21:1–4
- 'There will be a day' word collection
- copies of *The Big Bible Storybook* open at 'The city of God', or other children's Bibles and Bible story books containing a version of Revelation 21:1–4
- copies of Revelation 21:1–4 (CEV) or Bibles
- copies of the 'There will be a day' ET questions

Busy Zone
- junk modelling items
- masking tape
- sticking plasters
- copies of the 'There will be a day' ET questions

Quiet Zone

- a separate area where people can be alone with their thoughts and God
- 'There will be a day' image collection (optional)
- 'There will be a day' word collection (optional)
- copies of Revelation 21:1–4 (CEV) or Bibles
- copies of the 'There will be a day' ET questions

Share

As your time for exploring together draws to a close, invite your community to come back together into small groups of three to five. Suggest that they share their responses to the questions posed at the beginning.

Giving thanks

Invite the explorers to share their reflections with the wider community, drawing together their responses and noting any common themes that emerge. Conclude by reading Revelation 21:1–4 again (from the same Bible version used earlier). Then lead your community in a prayer, thanking God for all that he has revealed through this story. Encourage your community to continue their conversations about this story as they leave, and to take with them any artwork/writings/thoughts from the session.

Frequently asked questions

Does Explore Together negate the need for age-specific ministry?
The practice of Explore Together embodies the principle that a multigenerational community can engage with God's Word, learn from each other and grow together.

It is also true that within age-specific ministries there can be diversity of thought, rich experience and God-given creativity for sharing. Explore Together is a rare tool that can be used to nourish all-age community as well as enhance those ministries aimed at specific age-groups.

Although some churches do take and use Explore Together as a discrete part of their monthly programme, many churches use it to enrich their existing activities. The beauty of Explore Together is that it can be used within children's groups, youth groups, house groups, school groups, Bible study groups, outreach groups or even within the family home – in fact, anywhere that the Bible is shared. Its benefits are not restricted to all-age services.

We are a very traditional church community. How could Explore Together work within our traditions?
Explore Together embraces tradition but also pushes the boundaries that can be imposed by those traditions. It can fit neatly into the traditional order of things and can also be the catalyst that takes the community on an additional adventure.

Explore Together can be used to help people understand and interpret the meaning and value of symbol and tradition. A whole range of churches from a number of different traditions have taken and used it in different ways. It offers flexibility for churches and communities to make the time of exploring their own, using it so that it fits their group of people.

Our church has many people/a few people. Will it work here?
Over the last five years we have seen Explore Together used in small groups with only a few

individuals and also in larger settings. We have known Explore Together to be used within a family home, and also within a programme at Spring Harvest for 450 children.

Key to the smooth running of Explore Together are preparation and planning. It is important to consider how the participants will arrange themselves into small groups. There is a danger that individuals who are close friends, or of similar age and background, will organise themselves into groups, therefore missing out on the excellent opportunity to learn from those who are a different age or stage in their lives. Inclusivity is key if individuals want to be challenged to learn something new.

While the planning, organisation and setting up of the zones are essential, large or small numbers of people do not present a challenge. No matter how large the group is, Step 5: Share is always done in small groups of three to five people. When feeding back in larger churches or groups, having a group of people with roving radio microphones in the congregation works very well.

Isn't Explore Together a bit chaotic, especially with children present?
It is chaotic in the sense that everyone is engaging in different ways, but not because the children are present. The explore zones are designed to embrace a range of learning preferences. Individuals of all ages very quickly find their own preferred activity and become occupied. Although there might be a buzz in the room, activity will be purposeful, colourful and appealing, and everyone has the freedom to move around and make choices in a safe and supportive environment. Many adults find the kinaesthetic dimension of Explore Together appealing too!

Does Explore Together need a lot of space? We have fixed pews in our church building that often restrict what we can do.
Explore Together can be planned carefully to fit flexibly into spaces that are different in size and organised in different ways. The explore zones do not all need to happen in one room; they could be spread out to happen in different areas. Your choice of activities can

also be tailored to the amount of space you have, and you can creatively use the edges and corners of a room that contains pews. The smallest setting for Explore Together that we have heard about is at a dining room table in a family home.

I find sharing my ideas and thoughts very daunting. Do I really have to share my answers? Will others pressure me into talking?

The value of small groups is significant. Individuals have the opportunity to share what they have discovered, and shape the views, thinking and experiences of each other.

It is important that small groups are 'safe places', and that key expectations for how those groups will function are shared. Small groups need to be a place where individuals might not speak. There is huge value in being part of a small group and simply listening. Small groups also need to be a place where people can freely make mistakes; a place where original thoughts and ideas are encouraged. Some individuals might benefit from talking their ideas through one-to-one with another before sharing in a group, but others may never do so.

Individuals within groups need to be careful not to add to pressure others might feel. It should never be an expectation that everyone will talk.

Is Explore Together an alternative to Messy Church?

Messy Church and Explore Together complement each other in many ways. Explore Together can be used as a way of engaging with the Bible within any context. It is just one way of exploring the Bible 'in community'.

Messy Church is a Fresh Expression of church developed to encourage new congregations previously out of reach of 'traditional' church. Rather than replace Messy Church, Explore Together could be used within a Messy Church congregation. In his book *Making Disciples in Messy Church*, Paul Moore mentions that there is a lack of discipleship resources specifically designed for adults and children to use together in an all-age context, like Messy Church, or in the family home. I would strongly suggest that Explore Together ticks that box.

How inclusive is Explore Together for individuals with disabilities and learning difficulties?

Individuals with disabilities and learning difficulties have been involved in Explore Together since its inception. Those with physical difficulties, Down syndrome, diagnoses of ADHD and autistic spectrum disorder have all participated. Individuals are able to express their personal skills, interests and abilities in the explore zone. They can focus on tasks for a length of time that fits their capabilities, and they can share their answers in verbal and nonverbal ways.

It is important to eliminate barriers to participation when planning. For example, if your church or group has members with physical disabilities, it is a good idea to ensure that materials and activities are placed at a suitable height. For others, you might wish to use a visual timetable to help an individual know what will be happening next and to show the choices that are available to them in the explore zones.

Explore Together is a scary concept for our church. Is there any way we can implement it in stages?

The key to using Explore Together is to get to know and trust it. Using Explore Together in a smaller group setting to start with helps to build confidence and gets people involved. Using it in a house group setting or with a Sunday school group provides the ideal environment for becoming familiar with the process – children are so much more receptive to new ideas than adults!

I started using Explore Together with a small group of 5 to 11s. Other members of the children's team were involved and experienced first hand its effectiveness. From there we gained the confidence to share what we did in Sunday school with the wider church community. What started for me within a small group of children has now been used with 450 8 to 11-year-olds at Spring Harvest and in large national intergenerational events, too. If you need to, start small, but don't be afraid to grow.

How can Explore Together help adults who are reluctant to get out of the pew to engage?

The first thing to establish in situations like this is: Why the reluctance? If the reason concerns mobility and access then measures can be taken to make sure that all areas are easily available or, in extreme cases, the resources can be brought to the person.

More often than not the reluctance comes from the fear of change. The very nature of Explore Together is to provide an environment where every person can engage with the Bible in a way that embraces their natural preferences. There is quite literally something for everyone – the key is making sure that Explore Together is understood before it is forced upon a community that could be less than receptive.

If there are only one or two people for whom change may be difficult, take some time to sit down and explain what you plan to do and why you are doing it. There should be no pressure for people to go to a zone. One of the options is to reflect on the Bible passage quietly, and people could do this by staying in their seats; another is to deliver a sermon in the listening zone.

If the community is filled with people who are reluctant to leave their pews then maybe Explore Together in zone format is not right for you at this time. An alternative option would be to provide a bag (brown paper takeaway bags are ideal) for each person. The bag would contain a small notebook, a pen, a pack of coloured pencils, a small tub of play dough, some images relating to the Bible passage, a copy of the Bible passage or a Bible and a copy of the questions. The process would be the same, except that the community remains seated while they explore. The sharing time would be with those seated around them, and the feedback would happen in the same way as in the original format. This is less than ideal but it could be a stepping stone.

There will be a point at which a decision to move forward needs to be taken. Explore Together is a tool created to encourage people to discover the truths of the Bible for themselves. It is another pathway to a deeper relationship with God, intended to help people grow in their faith and reach maturity. Reluctance to engage should be seen as a pastoral opportunity to come alongside that person: to identify barriers and begin to break them down with prayer and persistence. Discipleship is never a done deal; it is a continuous journey that needs to take place in community. It also requires us to address and not ignore telltale signs that indicate the need for intervention – part of being a biblical community is to take that responsibility seriously (Colossians 1:28; 3:16). Explore Together helps to identify where on that journey we are and where help is needed.

What if someone says something completely off-the-wall?

My immediate response to this question is, 'it's better out than in'. What better place is there to explore your faith and ask your questions than in a community of faith – a community made up of many people with varying levels of understanding, wisdom, knowledge and experience? Explore Together provides a safe environment for people to express their thoughts and ideas, some of which may otherwise never be aired or challenged. The questions help to provide safe boundaries and keep the focus on the desirable aims and outcomes.

The web resources for the sessions in this book are available from:
www.exploretogether.org/downloads

Your access code is: 3Xp4rE6uRpL2